Pat C

GW01081203

UNDERSTANDING LOVE

Empathy in Relationships

VERITAS

First published 1999 by
Veritas Publications
7-8 Lower Abbey Street
Dublin 1

ISBN 1 85390 473 2

Cover design by Colette Dower
Cover photograph by Valerie O'Sullivan
Printed in Ireland by Paceprint Ltd, Dublin

*'To truly understand another human being,
you must first walk a mile in his moccasins.
And to do this you must first take off your own.'*

WHAT IS EMPATHIC LOVE?

In the Developing World, poverty is largely a material thing, in advanced countries like ours it is usually a psycho-spiritual phenomenon. In Western countries, the needs of the 'new poor' are hard to meet. 'The problems of the new poor', says Mother Teresa, 'are deep down, at the bottom of their hearts... here you have a different kind of poverty – a poverty of the spirit, of loneliness, and of being unwanted. And that is the worst disease in the world today, not tuberculosis or leprosy.' Many people share activities and tasks, but not themselves. Therefore it would probably be true to say that in individualistic cultures such as ours, love is the greatest need. As Mother Teresa puts it: 'People today are hungry for love, for understanding love, which is much greater and which is the only answer to loneliness and great poverty.'

Christian love as empathy

What is love? The 'silver rule' of the Old Testament stated: 'Do to no one what you would not done to you' (Jb 4:15). Jesus gave a clear, succinct reply when he advocated the 'golden rule' which has been esteemed in many cultures and religions: 'In everything do to others what you would have them do to you, for this sums up the Law and the Prophets' (Mt 7:12). In the post-resurrection era St Paul articulated the implications of this Christian precept. He knew that the heartfelt awareness of the love of God was the indispensable foundation of Christian ethics. As a result he prayed in Ephesians 3:17-19 that like him, all believers would be 'rooted and established in love' with the 'power to grasp how wide and long and high and deep is the love of Christ, and to know this love that surpasses knowledge.'

Once they are consciously aware of the love of God, believers were called to show that same love, as the first and foundational fruit of the Spirit (cf. Galatians 5:22) to others. As St Paul wrote in Romans 13:9-10: 'The commandments… are summed up in this one rule: 'Love your neighbour as yourself. Love does no harm to its neighbour. Therefore love is the fulfilment of the law.' In his famous hymn to love in 1 Corinthians 13:4-7, St Paul described some of the characteristics of loving generosity when he said: 'Love is patient, love is kind. It does not envy, it does not boast, it is not proud. It is not rude, it is not self-seeking, it is not easily angered, it keeps no record of wrongs. Love does not delight in evil but rejoices in the truth. It always protects, always trusts, always hopes, always perseveres.' To love, in this Christian way, two things are needed, *good will* and *insight*. A person with good will wants what's best for another. But that is not enough. Benevolence needs to be accompanied by an accurate awareness of the needs of the other person, which may be quite different from one's own.

For example, some time ago an anxious mother asked me to visit her son who had tried to commit suicide by taking an overdose. Apparently he had become very depressed following the death of a friend in a car accident. Although some of his despondency was due to grief, a lot of it was due to the fact that he was suppressing anger against his widowed mother. As a child he had developed a heart murmur following a bout of rheumatic fever. Afterwards, his mum had become very protective. She wouldn't allow him to play football, go out in cold weather, or take any kind of physical risks. She was so aware of her love that she presumed that she knew what was best for her son. In reality she had very little awareness of what it was like to be a young man with an overly protective mother, who, because of fear, wouldn't allow him to assert his independence. In spite of his repeated protests, she failed to sense the depth of his frustration or its causes. It was because he had to repress a lot of his resentment that he became dangerously downhearted. Arguably, in trying to protect her son's life, this loving but blinkered mother had contributed indirectly to his attempt to take his life. Good intentions are not enough. They need to be tempered by insight.

There are many ways of understanding and expressing Christian love in an insightful way. In recent years psychoanalysts, psychotherapists, counsellors and spiritual directors have emphasised the importance of empathy in therapy, and in loving relationships such as marriage and friendship. As a word empathy is relatively new in English. It was coined by Vernon Lee in 1904 from the Greek *en* in, and *pathos* feeling. Later the word was used to translate the German *einfühlung*, which literally means 'feeling into', which had first been used by R. H. Lotze in *Mikrokosmos* (1864). Some time later Theodor Lipps (1851-1914) used the word in the context of aesthetic appreciation. He described *einfühlung* as the act of projecting oneself into the object of perception, for example a painting, poem or piece of music, and sensing what feelings inspired the artist.

Empathy, therefore, is the intuitive process whereby one person sees the world from another person's perspective by sensing and understanding what he or she is experiencing. It enables the one who attends in this way to become aware – to a greater or lesser extent – of what the other person feels, perceives, values and believes. Gerard Egan defined empathy 'as the ability to enter and understand the world of another person and to communicate this understanding to him or her'. Incidentally, from a physiological point of view, it is thought that the amygdala, which is a part of the brain, is the organ that makes empathic emotional responses possible. Looked at more closely, empathic relationships have at least five characteristics.

1. By means of empathy a person becomes aware of the inner life of other people. It involves moment-by-moment sensitivity to the changing feelings which animate them – fear, rage, tenderness, confusion, joy, sorrow, longings etc.

2. Empathy seeks to understand other people's lives, by becoming aware of the unique perceptions, attitudes, values and beliefs that evoke their feelings, coloured as they are by their past experiences and memories. Arguably, this kind of understanding is facilitated by intuition and imagination. Etymologically, the word intuition literally means to 'see within'. By means of this spiritual gift, one can have an instinctive hunch or insight into the subjective experience of another person. One psychologist referred to it as vicarious introspection. It seems to me that it is facilitated by an ability to interpret body language. Current communications theory would indicate that, contrary to the common-sense impression that interpersonal communication is predominately verbal, about 80 per cent of it is actually conveyed by such things as subtle movements of facial muscles, dilation of the eyes, tone and pace of the voice, gestures, posture, mode of dress etc. These characteristics can mediate subjective states to intuitive people who are psychically sensitive. By means of imagination one can also project oneself into another's inner life by making a construct of what it might be like, based upon one's general psychological knowledge and personal experience.

3. Empathy studiously avoids judging, condemning or even

assessing other people's experiences in the light of abstract ideals or norms of perfection.

4. Empathic men and women mirror back their awareness of other people's feelings. It gives them the opportunity to establish whether their sense of their inner life is accurate or not. For example, a man who has failed to get a promotion describes his feelings. An empathic respondent might say, 'You really felt you deserved to get the job. So now you feel humiliated, disheartened and angry that a younger colleague got it instead.' Subsequently, good listeners are guided by the feedback they receive.

5. While empathic people don't share the feelings of others, they are not only aware of them, but they spontaneously respond to them at the emotional level. For example, a woman is aware of the hurt and anger of a grieving colleague who has had a miscarriage. While she doesn't share those emotions, the awareness of the other woman's plight evokes heartfelt feelings of tenderness and sadness within her.

Whereas empathy identifies what others feel, without necessarily sharing their experiences, sympathy does participate in those feelings. Although, etymologically the word literally means 'to suffer with', in modern English it has a wider connotation, and implies a willingness to share any kind of feeling (cf. Romans 12:15). In the seventeenth century St Vincent de Paul described this kind of sympathy when he said: 'One of the effects of love is to enable hearts to enter into each other and *feel what the other feels*.' Empathy or, indeed, sympathy for a person who is enduring suffering, for example of a psychological and emotional kind, is compassion.

DEGREES OF EMPATHY

Some psychologists have argued that there are four degrees of empathy.

Apathetic responses, are those where there is little or no identification with the feelings of others. So, strictly speaking, apathy is the absence of empathy. I know a woman who was badly injured when a stolen car, which was being driven by two teenaged boys, crashed into hers. She spent a long time in hospital, endured a lot of pain and afterwards had to cope with a permanent limp. The police gave the woman the names of the two young men who had caused her injuries. When she was released from hospital she called to their homes and explained to them what she had suffered as a result of the accident. Besides confronting them with the effects of their irresponsible behaviour, she hoped that they would regret what they had done and offer her an apology. In the event they were unmoved, and said in a callous, apathetic way, 'It's your problem, lady, not ours.'

Research has indicated that if empathy levels are high, people won't cause others pain and suffering, because in doing so they would be inflicting a portion of that pain on themselves. A number of studies in the 1970s have shown a link between high empathy and low delinquency. In his book *Emotional Intelligence*, Daniel Goleman has indicated that the outstanding characteristic of sociopaths, psychopaths and sexual molesters is the fact that they are devoid of empathy for their victims.

Familial empathy identifies with the feelings of relatives. Jesus may have had this kind of empathic love in mind when he said: 'If you, then, though you are evil, know how to give good gifts to your children, how much more will your Father in heaven give good gifts to those who ask him'! (Mt 7:11). The implication is that even self-centred people can display a surprising degree of loving empathy for their own next of kin. But that is as far as it goes. In the film Johnnie Brasco, Al Pacino plays the part of an ageing member of the Mafia. He becomes friendly with a younger man who, unbeknown to him, is an undercover cop. He explains to him that he has killed something like twenty-six people over the years and seems unmoved by the prospect of having to assassinate another. However, when his drug-addicted son is dangerously ill he shows great feeling for him.

Selective empathy, is extended to members of the same nationality, religion, class, sex etc. It has been obvious in Northern Ireland. Catholic Nationalists can feel for fellow Nationalists, and Protestant Unionists can feel for fellow Unionists when they suffer as a result of the troubles. However, I have noticed that their capacity to empathise is often restricted exclusively to members of their own communities. I can remember a time when a prominent Unionist politician was shot six times. Thank God he survived the attack. However, when word got round the town, many Catholic women banged the ground with dust-bin lids in a frenzy of celebration. When the man's wounded body was removed from the street someone drew an arrow, which pointed at a pool of his dried blood, and wrote, 'pig's blood'. Yet whenever a Nationalist was shot, there was weeping and gnashing of teeth. Surely Albert Nolan was correct when he stated in his book, *Jesus Before Christianity*, that our Lord believed that the human propensity to divide people into 'us' and 'them' was one of the principal sources of evil. 'Satan's kingdom,' he says, 'is based upon the exclusive and selfish solidarity of groups, whereas God's "kingdom" is based upon the all-inclusive solidarity of the human race.'

Universal empathy is extended to anyone and everyone

without exception. Jesus illustrates this kind of unrestricted empathy in the parable of the Good Samaritan. The priest and the Levite are apathetic in their response. They fail to respond to their fellow Jew who had been cruelly mugged and robbed. However, when a non-Jewish Samaritan comes across the unfortunate victim he is unhesitatingly moved to compassion and offers practical help and aftercare (cf. Luke 10:25-37).

At this point we can look at a memorable contemporary instance of this kind of universal empathy. It is estimated that up to twenty million citizens of the Union of Soviet Socialist Republics died as a result of the Second World War. In *A Precocious Autobiography* poet Yevgeny Yevtushenko recalls a wartime incident which is redolent with the compassion of the New Testament.

> In 1941 Mama took me back to Moscow. There I saw our enemies for the first time. If my memory serves me right, nearly twenty thousand German war prisoners were to be marched in a single column through the streets of Moscow. The pavement swarmed with onlookers, cordoned off by police and soldiers. The crowd were mostly women. Every one of them must have had a father or a husband, a brother or a son, killed by the Germans. They gazed with hatred in the direction from which the column was to appear. At last we saw it. The generals marched at the head, massive chins stuck out, lips pursed disdainfully, their whole demeanour meant to show superiority over their plebeian victors. The women were clenching their fists, the soldiers and policemen had all they could do to hold them back. All at once something happened to them. They saw the German soldiers, thin, unshaven, wearing dirty, blood-stained bandages,

hobbling on crutches or leaning on the shoulders of their comrades; the soldiers walked with their heads down. The street became dead silent – the only sound was the shuffling of boots and the thumping of crutches. Then I saw an elderly woman in broken-down boots push herself forward and touch a policeman's shoulder saying: 'Let me through.' There must have been something about her that made him step aside. She went up the column, took from inside her coat something wrapped in a coloured handkerchief and unfolded it. It was a crust of black bread. She pushed it awkwardly into the pocket of a soldier, so exhausted that he was tottering on his feet. And now suddenly from every side women were running towards the soldiers, pushing into their hands bread, cigarettes, whatever they had. The soldiers were no longer enemies. *They were people.*

In his thought-provoking book, *Violence Unveiled: Humanity at the Crossroads*, Gil Bailie argues that in terms of its historical effects 'empathy for victims is Christianity's cardinal virtue'. As a result, Christianity undermines the whole ideology of violence, by pointing unambiguously at the demonic origin of the aggression that crucified Jesus, the God-man. By acclaiming the victim as Lord, the Gospels slowly begin to awaken an empathy for victims everywhere, whether they belong to one's own circle of relationships or not. He believes that violence, as Yevtushenko's extract indicates, loses its legitimacy if and when this empathic perspective becomes so widespread that it is even extended to enemies (cf. Romans 5:8; Matthew 5:44; Luke 6:27).

Are women more empathic than men, as Yevtushenko's extract would suggest? Experience would suggest that they are. When one reads the papers it becomes obvious that most, though by no means all reported crimes, whether exploitative, sexual, violent or abusive, have been perpetrated by men. Research tends to confirm the general impression that men are not as empathic as women. Moir and Jessel write in *A Mind to Crime*: 'Women have a brain that feels – more than men's – much of what others feel, be it pain or joy, and the knowledge of the pain that can be inflicted on others militates against the commission of the deed – whether it is the defrauding of pensioners or the sabotage of a company and other people's jobs through embezzlement.'

Other authors have argued that men and women perceive the world differently. The extent to which it is a matter of nature or nurture need not concern us here. One can understand the difference between male and female ways of looking at things in terms of two sets of polarities. In general terms, men tend to be general and abstract, whereas women tend to be more concrete and personal in their approach to reality, and therefore more likely to be empathic. It is probable that hormones also have a role to play. Because they have testosterone only, males are more easily aggravated than females. This form of arousal tends to provoke antagonistic feelings of anger and aggression that negate the likelihood of empathy.

Loving empathy of the universal kind is of central importance in the Christian life as we have suggested. Nevertheless, many writers have maintained that it is relatively rare. The philosopher Simone Weil wrote: 'The love of our neighbour in all its fullness means being able to say: 'What are you going through?'…Nearly all those who think they have this capacity do not possess it.' Psychiatrist Frank Lake wrote in similar vein: 'Christian empathy, by which a man makes himself available to the Holy Spirit to feel for others far beyond his own experience or capacities, is as desirable as it is rare.'

TYPICAL EFFECTS OF EMPATHIC LOVE

Empathy can have a number of beneficial effects. As Jesuit psychiatrist James J. Gill has observed: 'The relationship between love and empathy is reciprocal: the more empathy a person has for another, the better the chance of love resulting. On the other hand, the more love that exists, the higher the likelihood that empathy will be displayed.'

A. Empathy facilitates intimacy

The word 'intimacy' literally means 'to publish, to make known that which is innermost'. In an intimate relationship, whether sexual or non-sexual, two things are required. Firstly there is a need for honest self-disclosure, whereby a person tells the truth, the whole truth, and nothing but the truth about him or herself. Secondly, there is need for empathic attention whereby the listener, whether a spouse, friend or counsellor, pays self-forgetful, empathic attention to the speaker's innermost self.

B. Empathy overcomes isolation

Most people carry around the baggage of their inner pain such as grief, hurts and shameful secrets. By reflecting back the main feelings and meanings they are aware of, empathic people help others, especially those who are suffering, to feel understood and, therefore, connected. This not only helps them to overcome painful feelings of loneliness and isolation, it also helps them to identify and understand their own experience more effectively.

C. Empathy increases self-esteem

Empathic people also enable others to feel valued and appreciated. By paying sustained, self-forgetful attention to the experience of another, a person says in a wordless way, 'I value you, I appreciate your dignity.' In a word, he or she helps others to feel loved, because love can be defined – in admittedly unromantic terms – as the will to approve the perceived and potential inner worth of a person. As Joseph Pieper has written: 'Love testifies to being in agreement, assenting, consenting, applauding, affirming, praising, glorifying and hailing.... All of them are expressions of the will and mean, I want you to exist.' In other words, empathy says, in a non-verbal way, 'I approve of you, I want you to live to the full and to thrive.' This natural sense of inalienable value is informed by an awareness that the other person is made in God's image, and that God's Spirit lives within him or her. Not surprisingly, this kind of natural and Christian approval increases self-acceptance and self-esteem.

D. Empathy enables people to heal and to grow

Empathic people sense the natural and supernatural potential that is present in the personalities of those they attend to, and they help them to acknowledge and develop it. More often than not they say, in non-verbal terms, 'Become what you are.' As Goethe once said: 'If we take people as they are, we make them worse. If we treat them as if they were what they ought to be, we help them to become what they are capable of becoming.' Although psychoanalysts, therapists and counsellors are guided by different, and often contradictory theories of personality, they all get good results. Research indicates that the common denominator in successful therapy is loving empathy.

Because it acknowledges people's value it has the ability to release the healing powers of the personality. This is a central belief informing Rogerian and Jungian counselling techniques. 'Unconditional positive regard' toward the 'client', expressed in a sincere and gentle way, enables him or her to accept that he or she is accepted, thereby enabling the neurotic civil war of the heart, the conflict between the acceptable and unacceptable self, to come to an end. As Carl Rogers observes: 'A person who is loved appreciatively, not possessively, blossoms and develops his own unique self. The person who loves non-possessively is himself enriched.'

E. Empathy affirms people

Empathy also affirms people. The word 'affirmation' comes from the Latin *affirmare*, 'to make strong'. Etymologically speaking it is virtually the same as the word 'comfort', which is derived from the Latin *con fortis*, which literally means 'with strength'. Empathy strengthens the personality. The Holy Spirit, the Comforter, is active in and through Christian identification with others. As Ephesians 3:16 says, it makes the innermost self grow strong. It is worth noting that while empathy will usually comfort its recipients it won't necessarily console them. Incidentally, research points strongly to the conclusion that a high degree of affirming empathy in a relationship is possibly the most important factor in bringing about learning and change.

F. Affective empathic love leads to effective action

Chuck Gallagher, one of the founders of Marriage Encounter, says that love can be looked at as either empathic relationship or as service of a practical kind. Ideally, service of others in the form of appropriate action should be the expression of empathic relationship rather than a substitute for it, as it commonly is. Once empathic people know the real needs of others, they have both the desire and the graced ability to respond sensitively to them in emotional and practical ways. The following true story illustrates some of these points in a poignant way.

Although Tom worked in a psychiatric hospital he had no professional training. As a nurse's aide he cleaned the rooms and helped around the wards by bringing trays, lifting patients and so on. Mary was the sickest person in the hospital. She was a psychotic who had needed ongoing care for the last eighteen years. Since her arrival she had never spoken to anyone or looked them in the eye. All day long she just sat in a rocking-chair and rocked back and forth with her head down. The doctors had tried every type of therapy, but without success.

Tom noticed this woman. He found another rocking-chair and pulled it over next to Mary's. By paying attention to her body language he began to sense the inner pain and profound mistrust that had imprisoned her. That evening he decided that during his meal break he would bring his dinner on a tray, sit in a chair, and rock beside Mary as he ate. He returned the next evening, and the next, and did the same. He even asked for permission to come in on his days off. In fact he came regularly every evening for six months, rocking beside Mary. She never responded. Finally one evening as Tom was getting up to leave, Mary looked him straight in the eye and said, 'Good-night, Tom.' After that she began to get well. Tom still came each evening and rocked beside her. Eventually she recovered completely and was released from the hospital.

I find that story strangely moving. Tom had empathy for

Mary. He was aware of the inner suffering that had cut her off from other people. Instinctively he knew that what she needed was consistent empathy of a committed, unconditional kind. As she sensed Tom's undemanding and accepting love, Mary began to trust, and to emerge, like a latter-day Lazarus, from the tomb of her inner hurts.

BLOCKS TO EMPATHY

There are many typical blocks to empathy.

A. Egocentricity
From a moral point of view lack of understanding love is rooted in wilful egocentricity, a tendency to be exclusively preoccupied with one's own needs, experiences, thoughts, feelings and desires. From a Christian point of view such a person has failed to die to self. D. H. Lawrence captured something of this mentality in one of his poems: 'How beastly the bourgeoisie is, especially the male of the species…. Let him meet a new emotion, let him be faced with another man's need, let him come home to a bit of moral difficulty, let life face him with a new demand on his understanding and then watch him go soggy, like a wet meringue. Watch him turn into a mess, either a fool or a bully.' Timidity which is rooted in unacknowledged self-absorption seems to be the cause. As Jesus said in John 12:24, 'Truly, truly I say to you, unless a grain of wheat falls into the earth and dies, *it remains alone.*'

B. Unresolved emotional pain
From an emotional point of view many people suffer from what has been referred to as the toothache of the heart, the distracting pain of unacknowledged, or unresolved inner hurts. It is usually rooted in the deprivations and traumas of the past. They commonly result in inner states such as separation anxiety, low self-esteem, chronic grief, phobic fears, angry resentment etc. These negative feelings can lead to either mistrustful isolation or clinging dependency.

- Those who are mistrustful tend to relate in an apathetic way. They prefer facts to feelings. They substitute good advice for emotional rapport. This is particularly true of men. When they are faced by the emotional pain of another they can see it as a problem to be solved rather than an inner state to be sensed and understood.

- Those who are dependent cling to others emotionally. They seek to be understood more than they seek to understand. They talk a lot about their own feelings, while being surprisingly uninterested in the feelings of the people they depend upon, unless of course, those feelings are about themselves. As one joke puts it, 'Well, that's enough about me, it's over to you now, what do you think about me!'

C. Excessive self-reference

When people with unresolved emotional problems listen to others, they often suffer from excessive self-reference. Their attention tends to boomerang back to themselves. Instead of entering into the unique experience of friends, colleagues and acquaintances, they tend to use their stories to remind them of the details of their own inner lives. As a result they will commonly say 'I know exactly how you feel, I went through a similar experience', while going on to recount the details at great length. So instead of listening to the other person, they end up getting him or her to listen to them.

D. Counter-transference

Related to this form of excessive self-reference is what people in the caring professions refer to as counter-transference. The notion is Freudian in origin and refers to the listener's unconscious reaction to the person who is sharing. The one sharing, especially in a therapeutic relationship with a counsellor or therapist, can transfer feelings on to the listener which may have been evoked at an earlier stage of the person's life. The transference is called positive when the feelings attached to the listener are those of love and admiration. Negative transference occurs when these feelings consist of hostility or envy. Counter-transference occurs when the listener comes to like or dislike the speaker because of a perceived similarity to significant people, for example parents or siblings, in the listener's own past life. Failure to recognise the operation of counter-transference, which has its roots in the unconscious, can inhibit empathy. This is a complex and specialised subject which space does not allow us to explore here.

E. A judgmental attitude

Empathy can also be suppressed by adopting an evaluative attitude to life. Instead of accepting experiences in a non-critical, non-judgmental way, moralistic people are inclined to assess them in terms of perfectionistic ideals. This lack of unconditional regard is conveyed in body language and phrases such as, 'What you ought... must... should... have to do, is such and such.' This kind of response is another way of saying in a discouraging manner, 'If only you were different – in other words better – than the way you are now!'

F. Prejudices

Prejudice of any kind is another impediment to empathy. The word is derived from the Latin *praejudicium*, a previous judgement. So instead of sensing the emotions of others as they are, prejudiced listeners can unwittingly interpret feelings and experiences in terms of preconceived ideas and stereotypes, for example of a sexual, racial, sectarian or religious kind. Most of these prejudices are largely unconscious and unrecognised. They lead people to filter and censor experience in accordance with their unexamined, and sometimes questionable frameworks of understanding.

G. Anger and resentment

Unresolved anger of the antagonistic, resentful kind is alien to empathy. People with unforgiving hearts cannot identify with the feelings of another person. Instead they tend to be judgmental, critical, condemnatory. They are inclined to amplify and exaggerate the faults of the other person. As a result, their negative and aggressive feelings prevent them from sensing what the other person is experiencing. Deep down they suspect that if they allowed themselves to understand what the other person is going through, such an insight might move them to forgive, something they don't want to do.

A number of years ago I attended a conference in Wales. During one of the breaks I got into conversation with Jane, an older woman who, unbeknown to me, happened to be a psychotherapist. I found myself telling her that I was saddened by the fact that the relationship between myself and my mother was not good. At one point Jane proposed that we do a role play, in which she would pretend to be my mother, and she invited me to tell her how I felt. Following initial reluctance, I decided to give it a go. Soon I was freely pouring out my mixed feelings of love and admiration, on the one hand, and frustration and resentment on the other. When I finished, Jane suggested that we reverse the roles. 'By now I know what you feel,' she said. 'I'll act your part, you can pretend to be your mother.' I adamantly refused, maintaining that it was a senseless thing to do. As we parted Jane said, 'Promise me one thing, spend some time reflecting on why you refused to reverse the roles.' When I went back to my room I did think about Jane's question. All of a sudden the answer came to me. If for a moment I allowed myself to empathise with my mother, to see things from her point of view, I'd realise how painful it must have been to have sincere good will for such a demanding, articulate and critical son as myself. As soon as I half allowed myself to sense what my mother felt, in an understanding way, my resentments began to melt away. Subsequently our relationship improved a good deal, although it was never perfect.

There was an important addendum to the story. A few years later, some time after my mother's death, I was at a conference in England. At the end of a long healing service, two lay people asked if I wanted some prayer myself. I didn't really, but to avoid hurting their feelings I reluctantly said 'Okay'. They asked what I'd like to be prayed for. Without much conviction I said, 'My relationship with my mother wasn't always great, pray about that.' As soon as they started to pray I got more than I bargained for. I had a vivid imaginative sense of my late father standing in front of me. He looked disconcertingly real. I said nothing, but he spoke to me. 'Pat, I was delighted when you were born. But as you grew, I found you hard to understand, you were too imaginative and creative for me. But be assured that I was proud of you. But I didn't always know how to express my feelings. I know I let you down, I know that I failed to give you the encouragement and affirmation you needed as a young man. But don't for a moment feel that I didn't love you, because I did. Please forgive me for the ways in which I failed you.' At the end of this vivid visionary experience I found myself whispering, 'Daddy, of course I forgive you.' With that, the experience ended.

Afterwards I realised that the Lord had indeed heard the prayer of the two lay people. I became consciously aware that although my father had always been physically present at home, like many other fathers, he wasn't always emotionally present. In some ways he had failed to affirm me as a male. As a result, I had unfairly switched me desire for affirmation on to my mother. When, not surprisingly, she failed to satisfy my need, I felt hurt and resentful. As a result of these two related experiences, I have come to see that if one desires to truly empathise with others one must cleanse the heart of resentment, especially against one's parents.

GROWING IN EMPATHY

There are a number of ways of growing in empathy. Before looking at them it is worth noting that the capacity to empathise is first developed in childhood. Parents and carers can help to nurture it in small boys and girls, especially by responding to them in an empathic way, with what Daniel Stern has referred to as 'attunement'. It is made possible by a willingness to listen empathetically to children, and thereby to become aware of their needs and emotions. This helps growing children to have a nascent ability to recognise what they feel and as a result to have a rudimentary sense of the feelings of others. Research indicates that if parents show that they are angry and upset when their children misbehave, by the age of six the children experience these distressing emotions and sense that it because they have offended against the rules, values and beliefs that are important to their parents. However, if children cannot feel the disapproval and upset of the parents they will experience little or no pain or distress, and the motivation to avoid wrongdoing will, as a consequence, be weaker. This is an important point which indicates that empathy plays a key role children's emerging ethical sense. Children who feel secure in the love and approval of their parents and carers are more likely to grow in self-awareness, to empathise, and to act in a loving way. Conversely, those who are neglected, who experience emotional abuse rather than empathy, are more likely to grow up delinquent. That is why criticism and put-downs need to be avoided and praise and encouragement should be given as often as possible. Needless to say, this guideline continues to be relevant in adult life.

Empathy presupposes a good deal of emotional self-awareness. The extent to which a person is aware of his or her feelings in an understanding way will largely determine the extent to which he or she will be able to empathise with others. To grow in this kind of self-knowledge means spending regular quiet times alone. By empathising with the deeper as opposed to the surface self, people can become increasingly aware of neglected or repressed desires and memories, together with their associated feelings, especially those of a painful and negative nature, such as worthlessness, loss, guilt, anger etc. Dream interpretation can be an important help in this regard. It enables people to become aware of unconscious feelings. Subsequently they can go on to own and understand them. As a result, they progressively grow in self-intimacy while making peace with their own pasts. As they do, they learn to trust their inner selves and their spontaneous capacity to tune into and react to the feelings of others.

Being empathic requires a number of relationship skills such as asking open-ended questions, reflecting back the principal feelings, noticing and bracketing one's own emotions etc. Increasing awareness of the ways in which things such as body language intimate what people feel, can provide valuable clues about the subjectivity of others. As Freud wrote: 'He who has eyes to see and ears to hear, becomes convinced that mortals can keep no secret. If their lips are silent they gossip with their fingertips; betrayal forces its way through every pore.' However, skills such as these are only acquired with difficulty and with the help of others, for example by doing a counselling course. Even then, skills without genuine empathy are merely technique, while empathy without skill can be relatively ineffective.

Contemplating the empathy of Jesus

We know from the gospels that Jesus was compassionate and empathised with the people he met. When reading and praying the scriptures, Christians can try to empathise with the characters mentioned in the text, but most especially with our Lord. The Ignatian method, which appeals to the imagination, and the Benedictine method, which appeals to the rational mind, can be particularly helpful in this regard. The aim of both methods is to forget about oneself in order to concentrate on Jesus and to sense what he felt and experienced in his relationships with other people.

One begins this form of scripture mediation with a prayer, for example: 'In the scriptures, by the Spirit, may I see the Saviour's face, hear his word and heed his calling, know his will and grow in grace.' Then one goes on to choose a scripture passage, from the liturgy, or from the Bible, such as the story of the meeting between Jesus and the Samaritan woman at the well of Sychar in John 4:7-42.

- Imagine the scene, see the well, the village in the distance and Jesus and the woman. You might want to place yourself in the picture as an onlooker.

- Hear what is said by Jesus and the woman, and later by the disciples and townspeople.

- Notice what they do, for example, the woman self-consciously drawing up a pail of water from the well.

- Empathise with the emotions of the woman, but more especially with those of Jesus. Try to get inside his skin, so to speak, in order to sense what he felt as he related to her. Empathy, as we have seen, has five characteristics.
  1. By means of empathy one person becomes aware of the inner life of another. It involves moment-by-moment

sensitivity to the changing feelings which animate other people.

2. Empathy seeks to understand other people's lives, by becoming aware of the unique perceptions, attitudes, values, and beliefs that evoke their feelings, coloured as they are by their past experiences and memories.

3. Empathy studiously avoids judging, condemning or even assessing other people's experiences in the light of abstract ideals or norms of perfection.

4. Empathic men and women mirror back their awareness of other people's feelings. It means checking frequently with them as to whether their sense of their experience is accurate or not.

5. Although empathic people don't share the feelings of others, they are not only aware of them, but respond to them at the emotional level.

As you read and meditate on the encounter between Jesus and the Samaritan at the well, you might advert to the characteristics of empathy just mentioned. Notice how Jesus illustrates each one of them in his conversation with the woman.

1. He seems to be aware of her mistrust, loneliness, sense of shame, and longing to be loved, to feel special to someone, to belong.

2. He understands the reasons for her feelings. He senses that she has looked in vain for such love in the arms and beds of a number of men. Instead of finding lasting intimacy she has been ostracised because of her permissive sexual behaviour.

3. He does not condemn or lecture her in any way. He shows this by breaking a number of taboos by talking to her – a

woman, a Samaritan woman – and defying the ritual laws of purity by asking her for a drink.

4. He reflects back his sense of her innermost feelings and desires by talking in a symbolic way about the living water of the Spirit that will truly satisfy her.

5. While he doesn't share the woman's feelings, he responds to them with tenderness, compassion and sensitivity.

You could use this method for many other gospel accounts which describe Jesus' interaction with the different people he met. In this way you can get to know who Jesus is and what he is like. As the *Catechism of the Catholic Church* says in a profound and moving manner 'Christ enables us to live in him all that he himself lived, and to live it in us' (§521). Those who meditate in this prayerful way are thereby motivated to die to egocentricity so that they may live for God through loving, empathic relationships with their neighbours. There are many aspects to this purgative process. Suffice it to say, that among other things it requires a daily *decision* to live, with the grace of God, in accordance with the Golden Rule. As St Paul has assured us: 'It is God who works in you to will and to act according to his good purpose' (Ph 2:13).

Conclusion

Loving empathy is of central importance in the Christian life as we have suggested. The German theologian Dietrich Bonhoeffer said that the first service one owes to others in the community consists in listening to them. Just as love of God begins by listening to his Word, so the beginning of love for others is learning to listening empathetically to them. Many people are looking for an ear that will listen. All too often, they fail to find it among Christians, because they are too busy talking where they should be paying attention. But the person who can no longer listen to others will soon not be listening to God either, he or she will do nothing but prattle in the presence of God. This is the beginning of death as far as the spiritual life is concerned.

With these sentiments in mind, it is interesting to note that people who have had near-death experiences testify that, having passed through a dark tunnel, they were invited to evaluate their lives in the light of Divine Love and the Golden Rule. Dr Raymond Moody, author of *Life after Life*, said in an interview: 'Patients often report that during their life review they view the events of their lives not from the perspective that they had when they went through the event, but rather from the third person perspective. Their perspective is displaced, and as they watch themselves go through these life actions, they can also empathetically relate to the people with whom they have interacted. They take the perspective of the person they have been unkind to. And if they see an action where they have been loving to someone, then they can feel the warmth and good feelings that they produced in the life of that person.' It would appear, therefore, that in the autumn of our lives we will be judged largely – as Matthew 25:31-46 suggests – on the basis of empathic love.